Bildschöner
SCHWARZWALD

Klaus-Jürgen Vetter (Herausgeber)

INHALT · CONTENT

◄◄ **BLICK ÜBER DEN MUMMELSEE.** Der See liegt an der Schwarzwaldhochstraße am Fuß der Hornisgrinde.
◄◄ **VIEW UPON LAKE MUMMELSEE.** The lake lies at the foot of the Hornisgrinde.

◄ **GÜTENBACH** im geheimnisvollen Morgenlicht. Der kleine Ort befindet sich in der Nähe von Furtwangen.
◄ **GÜTENBACH** in mysterious morning light. The little town is located near Furtwangen.

„Von Baden-Baden aus begaben wir uns auf den üblichen Abstecher in den Schwarzwald. Die meiste Zeit waren wir zu Fuß. Man kann diese edlen Wälder nicht beschreiben, noch die Gefühle wiedergeben, zu denen sie inspirieren."

"From Baden-Baden we made the customary trip into the Black Forest. We were on foot most of the time. One cannot describe those noble woods, nor the feeling with which they inspire him."

Mark Twain (1835–1910)
A Tramp Abroad

DER SCHWARZWALD ist das höchste deutsche Mittelgebirge, der Feldberg bildet mit 1493 Metern über dem Meer die höchste Landmarke Deutschlands außerhalb der Alpen. Auf einer Länge von rund 170 Kilometern erstreckt sich der Schwarzwald vom Durlacher Turmberg in Karlsruhe südwärts bis zum Hochrhein, im Westen erheben sich seine felsendurchsetzten Flanken aus der sonnigen Oberrheinebene, nach Osten zu flacht er sanft zu den Gäuflächen der Baar und Württembergs ab. Schon in der Antike waren die Heilquellen dieses Gebirges bekannt. Seine größte Breite und Höhe erreicht der Schwarzwald im Süden, wo er im Feldberg gipfelt und sich 60 Kilometer von Müllheim im Markgräflerland bis zur Wutach, einem der eindrucksvollsten Schluchtensysteme Deutschlands, erstreckt. Das Foto zeigt Obstbaumfluren rund um Obereggenen im Markgräflerland.

THE BLACK FOREST is the highest region of the Central German Uplands, and with 1493 meters above sea level, the Feldberg is Germany's highest landmark outside the Alps. Running a length of approximately 170 kilometers, the Black Forest stretches from Durlacher Turmberg in Karlsruhe southward up to Hochrhein, in the west its cliff-riddled slopes reach up from the sunny Upper Rhein area, in the eastward direction it flattens out gently to the arable fields of the Baar and Württemberg. Already in ancient times, the mineral springs were known. The Black Forest reaches its greatest breadth and height in the South, where it reaches its peak in Feldberg and stretches 60 kilometers from Müllheim in Markgraeflerland to Wutach, one of the most impressive canyon systems in Germany. The photo shows fruit tree woodland surrounding Obereggenen in Markgräflerland.

▶▶ Bollenhut und Kuckucksuhr, Vogtsbauernhof und Schwarzwaldbahn: Viele Schwarzwald-Markenzeichen stammen aus dem mittleren Schwarzwald. Der aus dem Gutachtal stammende Bollenhut wurde zum Inbegriff der Schwarzwald-tracht: ein Strohhut mit roten Wollbällen („Bollen") für Mädchen und schwarzen Bällen für verheiratete Frauen. Die Gutacher Mädchen (oben links) prangen im Erntedank-Schmuck. Um 1800 entstand diese Tracht in den lutherischen Gemeinden des Gutachtals, um sich von den Trachten der Katholiken des Umlands zu unterscheiden. Mit dem Vogtsbauernhof verfügt das Gutachtal zudem über das meistbesuchte Freilichtmuseum des Schwarzwalds: Es präsentiert fünf der sieben Schwarzwaldhaus-Typen mit Originaleinrichtung. Rund um den 400 Jahre alten Vogtsbauernhof wurden weitere Höfe des 16. –- 18. Jahrhunderts aus dem mittleren und Nordschwarzwald hierher versetzt.

▶▶ The traditional hat, the "Bollenhut," and the cuckoo-clock, the Open Air Museum Vogtsbauernhof and the Black Forest Railway: Many Black Forest landmarks are from the central region. The Bollenhut, originating from Gutachtal, came to epitomize the traditional Black Forest dress: a straw hat with red woollen balls ("Bollen") for girls and black balls for married women. The Gutach girls (above on the left) are resplendent in their Thanksgiving attire. In around 1800, this traditional dress originated in the Lutheran communities of the Gutach Valley, as a mark of differentiation from the traditional dress of the surrounding Catholic areas. With the Vogtsbauernhof, the Gutach Valley also has the most frequented open air museum of the Black Forest: It presents five of the seven types of houses with original furnishings. Surrounding the 400-year-old Vogtsbauernhof, further farm houses from the other parts of the Black Forest have been transplanted here.

◄ **NATURPARKS.** Der Geroldsauer Wasserfall bei Baden-Baden ist eine der Perlen, denen der Schwarzwald seinen Naturparkstatus verdankt. Nahezu der gesamte Schwarzwald ist dank seiner Naturwunder, ökologischen Vielfalt und reichen Kultur – das Foto unten zeigt einen Bauernhof bei Todtnau im Südschwarzwald – als Naturpark ausgewiesen: Der „Naturpark Schwarzwald Nord/Mitte" ist mit 3600 Quadratkilometern der größte Naturpark in Deutschland, gefolgt vom „Naturpark Südschwarzwald" (3300 km²), der nahtlos an ihn anschließt. Die Schönheit des Schwarzwalds lässt sich in allen Regionen erleben: Faszinierende Eisenbahnlinien wie die Höllentalbahn, Ferienrouten wie die Deutsche Uhrenstraße erschließen Panoramaberge, Burgen, Fachwerkorte, Klöster und Bäder ebenso wie der Schwarzwald-Radweg oder der Westweg als bedeutendster Höhen-Fernwanderweg. Ob im Hochseilgarten oder schwebend am Gleitschirm, ob in einem der vielen Museen oder bei Hirschrückenfilet und badischem Wein: Der Schwarzwald ist immer ein Erlebnis.

◄ **NATURAL PRESERVES.** The Geroldsau waterfall near Baden-Baden is one of the gems responsible for the Black Forest's status as a natural preserve. Thanks to its natural beauty and rich culture – the photo below depicts a farmhouse near Todtnau in the southern Black Forest – nearly the entire Black Forest has been designated as a natural preserve: The "Naturpark Schwarzwald Nord/Mitte," with its 3600 km², is the largest natural preserve in Germany, followed by "Naturpark Südschwarzwald" (3300 km²), bordering each other seamlessly. The beauty of the Black Forest can be experienced in all its regions: Fascinating railway lines, such as the Hoellen Valley railway, or vacationing routes, such as the German Uhrenstraße, make accessible the panorama mountains, fortresses, towns with half-timbered houses, monasteries and spas, just as with the Black Forest bicycle path or the Westweg hiking trail. Whether in one of the countless museums or at one of the stately guest houses with a saddle of venison filet and a Badish regional wine: The possibilities of experiences in the Black Forest is limitless.

DER NATURPARK SÜDSCHWARZWALD erstreckt sich in der sonnenverwöhntesten Region Deutschlands zwischen dem Kaiserstuhl an der Grenze zu Frankreich und dem Hochrheintal an der Grenze zur Schweiz, zwischen der Wutachschlucht und den Triberger Wasserfällen, den höchsten Wasserfällen der Republik – ein Gebirge der Superlative, das im Feldberg gipfelt, dem höchsten Berg aller deutschen Mittelgebirge. Von spektakulären Felsszenerien und wasserfalldurchbrausten Schluchten spannt sich der Bogen seiner Naturparadiese bis hin zu den Pflanzenoasen auf Feldberg, Herzogenhorn und Belchen, von Urwäldern, romantischen Seen und den Quellen der Donau bis hin zu Wallfahrtsorten mit Alpenblick. Zugleich ist es ein Kulturparadies, in dem sich im Dreiländereck Deutschland, Frankreich und die Schweiz facettenreich begegnen – wie beim gemütlichen Beisammensein im Biergarten hoch über Freiburg.

THE SOUTH BLACK FOREST NATURAL PRESERVE, in the sunniest region of Germany, extends between the Kaiserstuhl on the border to France and the High Rhine Valley on the border to Switzerland, between the Wutach Canyon and the Triberg Waterfalls, the republic's highest waterfalls – a mountain range of superlatives, climaxing in the panoramic Feldberg, the highest mountain of all the Central German Uplands. From the spectacular cliff scenery and canyon roaring with waterfalls, its natural paradise spans all the way to the oasis of vegetation on Feldberg, Herzogenhorn and Belchen, from the primeval forests, romantic lakes and the spring of the Danube all the way to the pilgrimage sites with a view of the Alps. At the same time, the Black Forest is truly a cultural paradise, in which the border triangle Germany, France and Switzerland meets in its variety – as in a cosy get-together in a beer garden high above Freiburg.

FREIBURG IM BREISGAU ist die „Hauptstadt" des Süd-schwarzwalds. Die historische Altstadt mit dem gotischen Münster und den bächledurchflossenen Gassen zählt zu den schönsten im deutschen Südwesten. Bereits 1457 wurde die traditionsreiche Albert-Ludwigs-Universität gegründet. Der Schlossberg, auf dem Herzog Berthold II. von Zähringen 1091 die Hauptburg der Zähringer errichten ließ, bietet einen hervorragenden Blick auf das gotische Schwabentor (Foto rechts). Das Colombischlösschen (oben links) in einem eng-lischen Garten am Rotteckring beherbergt das Museum für Ur- und Frühgeschichte. Vor dem Münster erstreckt sich der Marktplatz (oben rechts), Wirtschaften (unten links) laden in der autofreien Altstadt zum Verweilen ein. Das Martinstor (1202, unten rechts) ist der älteste erhaltene Wehr- und Tor-turm der mittelalterlichen Stadtbefestigung.

FREIBURG IN BREISGAU is the "capital city" of the South Black Forest. The historical city center, with its Gothic cathe-dral and the brook-lined lanes, is among the most beautiful in the south-west of Germany. The traditional Albert Ludwig University was already founded in the year 1457. The Schloss-berg, upon which Duke Berthold II of Zähringen had the main fortress of Zähringen's citizens built in 1091, offers an exquisite view of the Gothic Schwabentor (photo on the right). The Colombi Castle (upper left), in an English garden at the Rotteckring, houses the Museum for Prehistoric and Early History. The market place is spread out before the cathedral (upper right), Eating and drinking establishments (lower left) invite one to relax in the auto-free city center. The Martinstor (1202, lower right) is the oldest preserved defense and gate tower of the medieval city fortifications.

◄ DIE FREIBURGER ALTSTADT besticht durch die Vielzahl historischer Bauwerke, die Straßen und Gassen sind weitgehend Fußgängerzone und präsentieren sich weltoffen, was auch in der Sprachenvielfalt aus Schwäbisch, Alemannisch, Elsässisch, Französisch und Schwyzerdütsch fühlbar wird. Am Marktplatz (oben links) stehen der rote Renaissancebau des Alten Rathauses und der im 19. Jahrhundert errichtete weiße Bau des Neuen Rathauses (oben rechts). Das Historische Kaufhaus (Mitte rechts) am Münsterplatz war im Mittelalter die Schaltstelle des Waren- und Finanzverkehrs. 1368 erhielt Freiburg das Münzrecht; die heutige Münzgasse (unten rechts) erinnert daran. Der Kanonenplatz unterhalb des Burgfelsens bietet eine herrliche Aussicht und ist beliebtes Ziel von Ausflüglern und Radwanderern (unten links).

◄ THE FREIBURG CITY center impresses visitors with its numerous historical structures, the auto-free streets and lanes captivate with their cosmopolitan flair, which can also be felt in the diversity of the languages spoken: Swabian, Alemannic, Alsatian, French and Swiss German. At the market place (upper left) stand the red Renaissance building of the Old City Hall and the white building of the New City Hall (upper right), built in the 19th century. The historical department store (right center) on the cathedral square was the center of commercial and financial activity in the middle ages. In 1368, Freiburg was granted the regional right to mint and issue coins; today the former mint street (lower right) attracts those out for a stroll, with its bars and cafés. The canon square below the fortress cliffs, with its wonderful view, is a favourite spot for those taking excursions and on cycling tours (below left).

◄ DER FREIBURGER MÜNSTERTURM – im Bild jenseits der Alten Universität – gilt als schönster Turm der Christenheit. Der Aufstieg in diesem Meisterwerk der Gotik und die Ausblicke sind die Krönung des Münsterbesuchs. In den 1280er-Jahren holten sich die Freiburger Bürger einen neuen Baumeister: Er setzte auf den Unterbau den filigranen Turmhelm, im Einklang mit der damaligen Erlebnismystik konzipiert als Aufstiegsweg in eine göttliche Wirklichkeit über den Wolken. Finanziert wurde das Münster von den Bürgern einer mittelalterlichen 8000-Einwohner-Stadt. Für den Bau der Kirche „Unserer lieben Frau" spendeten sie überreichlich, sie beriefen Baumeister und Künstler, auch die Silberausbeute der Schauinsland-Bergwerke trug zur Finanzierung bei. Den Bombenhagel des Jahres 1944 überstand das Münster wie durch ein Wunder unversehrt.

▼ DAS HOTEL „ZUM ROTEN BÄREN" in der Salzstraße nimmt für sich in Anspruch, der älteste Gasthof in Deutschland zu sein. Die Fundamente des „Bären" stammen aus der Zeit vor der Stadtgründung 1120.

◄ THE FREIBURG MINSTER TOWER – depicted in the photo beyond the Old University – is considered the most beautiful tower of Christendom. Ascending this light-filled Gothic masterpiece is the highlight of any cathedral visit. In the time of the 1280s, during the period of Female Mysticism, the citizens of appointed a new master builder: Upon the foundation, he set a filligreed, open work spire, in keeping with the era's experiential mysticism, conceived as an ascending path into a devine reality above the clouds. The Minster was financed by the citizens of medieval city with a population of 8000. For the construction of the "Unserer lieben Frau" church, they donated money and all kjionds of valuable, they appointed master builder and artists, and the silver obtained from the Schauinsland mine substantially contributed to the financing. The Minster miraculously withstood the air bombings of the year 1944.

▼ THE "ZUM ROTEN BÄREN" HOTEL claims itself to be the oldest guesthouse in Germany. Its foundations originate even before the time of the city's founding in 1120.

◄◄ SANKT PETER hat die bedeutendste Klosteranlage im Breisgau bewahrt. Der habsburgische Architekt Peter Thumb errichtete 1724–27 als Teil des Klostergevierts die spätbarocke Kirche, deren markante Doppelturmfassade majestätisch über dem heutigen Luftkurort thront: Wer sie betritt, steht in einem weißen Raum aus Licht, Stuckaturen, Altären. Ein Juwel ist auch die von Joseph Feuchtmayer ausgestattete Rokokobibliothek des Klosters (oben rechts). Herzog Berthold II. von Zähringen verlegte nach seiner Wahl zum Gegenherzog von Schwaben das zähringische Hauskloster Sankt Peter von Weilheim an der Teck auf den Schwarzwald in die Berge des Breisgaus, die feierliche Weihe fand am 1. August 1093 statt.

SAINT PETER has preserved the most important monastery complex in Breisgau. In the years 1724–27, the Habsburg architect Peter Thumb erected, as part of the cloister of the late baroque church, whose distinctive twin-tower façade stands in majestic spender over the contemporary climatic health resort: Those who enter stand in a white room of light, ornamental plasterwork, alters. The rococo library (upper right) furnished by Joseph Feuchtmayer is also a treasure. Duke Berthold II of Zähringen moved the Zähringen house cloister Saint Peter from Weilheim an der Teck to the Black Forest, in the mountains of Breisgau, and the celebratory consecration took place on August 1, 1093.

◄ DAS LANDSCHAFTSIDYLL von Sankt Peter ist ein Dorado für Wanderungen mit Blick auf die höchsten Schwarzwaldberge sowie bei Inversionswetterlage sogar bis zu den Alpen.

THE IDYLLIC COUNTRYSIDE of Saint Peter is an El Dorado for hiking, with a view of the highest Black Forest mountains, as well as the alps, with inverted atmospheric conditions.

◄◄ Die alleeartige „Römerstrasse" zählt zu den beliebtesten Wanderwegen über dem Dreisamtal, das Foto zeigt den Blick auf die doppeltürmige Wallfahrtskirche von Sankt Märgen. Der bequeme Höhenweg zwischen Sankt Märgen und Sankt Peter führt an der Rankmühle (links unten) vorbei und weiter am Waldrand mit herrlichen Ausblicken über alte Gehöfte hinweg bis zu den höchsten Bergen des Südschwarzwalds (oben rechts).

Like a romantic lane, the "Römerstraße" is among the best loved hiking paths over the Dreisam Valley, and the photo depicts a view of the pilgrimage church with twin towers, Saint Märgen. The high path stretching between Saint Märgen and Saint Peter leads past the Rankmühle (lower left), and further on past the forest edge and beyond, to the highest mountains of the southern Black Forests (upper right).

◄ Der Höhenluftkurort Breitnau erstreckt sich als Streusiedlung mit zahlreichen alten Gehöften vom Höllental und der Ravennaschlucht bis hinauf zur Weißtannenhöhe.

The high altitude health resort of Breitnau extends as a scattered settlement, with numerous old farmsteads from Höllen Valley and the Ravenna Canyon all the way up to the Weißtannenhöhe.

◄ Im Oberfallengrundhof bei Neukirch erblickte der Rokokobildhauer Mathias Faller (1707–91) das Licht der Welt. Seine letzte Ruhestätte fand der „Herrgottschnitzer des Schwarzwalds" in der Marienkapelle des Klosters Sankt Märgen.

It was in Oberfallengrundhof near Neukirch that rococo sculpture Mathias Faller (1707–91) first saw the light of day. The final resting place of the "Crucifix Carver of the Black Forest" is found in the Marienkapelle (Chapel of Our Lady) of the Saint Märgen Monastery.

◄◄ DIE TRIBERGER WASSERFÄLLE sind die höchsten Wasserfälle der deutschen Mittelgebirge. In sieben Kaskaden stürzt die Gutach 163 Meter über schroffe Granitfelsen, während der Schneeschmelze und nach starken Regenfällen tosen enorme Wassermassen durch das schluchtartig eingeschnittene Tal.

THE TRIBERG WATERFALLS form the highest waterfall of the Central German Uplands. In seven cascades, the Gutach River plummets 163 meter over craggy granite cliffs, and during the melting season and after strong rains, it roars in enormous floods of water through the canyon-like valley.

▲ DAS RAVENNAVIADUKT der Höllentalbahn von Freiburg nach Donaueschingen überspannt seit 1927 auf 224 Metern Länge und bis zu 40 Metern Höhe die Ausmündung der Ravennaschlucht.

THE RAVENNA VIADUCT of the Höllen Valley railway from Freiburg to Donaueschingen spans the mouth of the Ravenna Canyon since 1927, with a length of 224 meter and a heigh of up to 40 meter.

◄ DIE HEXENLOCHMÜHLE bei Neukirch ist die Bilderbuch-Wassermühle des Südschwarzwalds. Erbaut wurde sie 1825 als Sägemühle, seit 1839 befindet sie sich im Besitz der Familie Trenkle, die hier ein Gasthaus betreibt und Schwarzwälder Spezialitäten anbietet.

THE HEXENLOCHMÜHLE near Neukirch is the picture book watermill of the southern Black Forest. It was built in 1825 as a sawmill, and since 1839 owned by the family Trenkle, who run a guesthouse here and sell Black Forest specialties.

◄ DER BALZER HERRGOTT ist eine Christusfigur, die in eine rund 300 Jahre alte Buche einwächst.

THE BALZER HERRGOTT is a depiction of Christ, grown into a circa 300-year-old beech tree.

▼ DIE RESIDENZSTADT DONAUESCHINGEN liegt auf der Hochfläche der Baar am Zusammenfluss von Brigach und Breg zur Donau. Das Fürstlich Fürstenbergische Schloss (ab 1723) erhielt seine neobarocke Gestalt durch einen Umbau 1893 im Stil der Belle Époque und beherbergt heute ein Museum zur fürstlichen Wohnkultur des 17. bis 19. Jahrhunderts. Die „Donauquelle" im Park vor dem Schloss ist eine der meistbesuchten Quellen Europas.

▼▼ VILLINGEN hat seinen mittelalterlichen Altstadtkern bewahrt. Herzog Berthold III. ließ die Stadt ab 1119 planmäßig nach dem für Zähringer Städte typischen Kreuzgrundriss anlegen und das später gotisierte Münster „Unserer lieben Frau" (unten links) errichten. Im 13. Jahrhundert kam die Stadtmauer mit den Stadttoren und Wehrtürmen hinzu (unten rechts: Riettor; rechts: Fassade in der Rietstraße).

▼ THE ROYAL SEAT OF DONAUESCHINGEN lies on the plateau of the Baar, at the confluence of the Brigach and Breg to the Danube. The princely Fürstenberg Castle (from 1723) was given its neo-baroque design during its modification in 1893 in the style of the Belle Epoque, and today it houses a museum with collections of the princely home décor of the 17th to 19th centuries. The "Donauquelle" in front of the castle is one of Europe's most frequently visited springs.

▼▼ VILLINGEN has maintained its city center since the Middle Ages. Beginning in 1119, Duke Berthold III had the city built according to the cross-shaped ground plan, typical of Zähringen cities, as well as the later Gothic "Unserer lieben Frau" Minster (lower left). In the 13th century, the preserved city wall with the city gates and defence towers were added (below right: Riettor, right side: façade in Riestraße).

◀◀ **BREISACH** liegt auf einem vulkanischen Auslieger des Kaiserstuhls an einem schon in der Antike genutzten Rheinübergang. Wahrzeichen ist das gotische Stephansmünster. Es birgt unter anderem das Gerichts-Triptychon von Martin Schongauer (1488–91, Fresko).
BREISACH lies on a volcanic outlier of the Kaiserstuhl, at a crossing of the Rhine already used in ancient times. Its symbol is the Gothic Stephan's Minster. It houses the judgement triptych by Martin Schongauer (1488–91, fresco).

▲ **BADENWEILER** ist einer der ältesten Thermalkurorte Deutschlands und verfügt über die größte und am besten erhaltene römische Thermenruine nördlich der Alpen. Die Ruinen des römischen Bads befinden sich im Kurpark, die Cassiopeia Therme (oben) ist das heutige Wellness-Zentrum.
BADENWEILER is one of the oldest thermal health resorts of Germany, and has the largest and best preserved Roman thermal ruins this side of the Alps. The ruins of the roman bath are embedded in the health resort, while the main spa center today is the "Cassiopeia Therme" (upper right).

◀ **IN STAUFEN** ereignete sich im Jahr 1539 im „Gasthaus zum Löwen" (das rosa Gebäude) ein Unglück, das bis heute in Musik und Literatur weiterlebt: Der Alchemist und Magier Dr. Johannes Faust wurde beim Versuch, für den Freiherrn von Staufen Gold zu brauen, angeblich vom Teufel geholt – rußschwarz lag der Entseelte nach einer Explosion auf dem Boden.
A TERRIBLE ACCIDENT occurred in Staufen in the year 1539, in the "Gasthaus zum Löwen" (the rose-colored building), which today lives on in music and literature: The alchemist and sorcerer Dr. Johannes Faust was taken by the devil, during an attempt to brew gold for the Baron von Staufen – the soulless one lay soot-black on the floor, following an explosion.

► BURKHEIM ist eine mittelalterlich ge-
prägte Weinstadt auf einem Bergsporn des
Kaiserstuhls oberhalb der Rheinauen. Nach
der Erhebung zur Stadt im 12. Jahrhundert
wurde die Wehrmauer um die „Mittelstadt"
errichtet. Das nordöstliche Stadttor mit
dem Mansarddach erhielt seine heutige Gestalt beim Wiederaufbau unter habsburgi-
scher Herrschaft im 18. Jahrhundert. In der
Mittelstadt mit ihren Massiv- und Fach-
werkbauten, ihren reich verzierten Erkern
lebten die Winzer und Kaufleute, in der Vor-
stadt die Rheinfischer. Heute gehört Burkheim zu Vogtsburg.

BURKHEIM is a wine city, marked by the
Middle Ages, on a cliff of the Kaiserstuhl
up from the Rhine Falls. After attaining city
status in the 12th century, the defence wall
was erected around the "middle city." The
north-east city gate with the Mansarddach
took on its current design during recon-
struction under Habsburg rule in the 18th
century. The middle city, with its massive
and timbered structures, its richly decorat-
ed oriels lived the winery owners and mer-
chants; in the outskirts lived the Rhine
fishermen. Today, Burkheim is part of the
city of Vogtsburg.

►► ÜBER BURKHEIM HINWEG schweift
der Blick zu den Hochlagen des Kaiserstuhls. Die im Lauf von Jahrhunderten ent-
standene Pfarrkirche wird schon um das
Jahr 1000 als „Basilica S. Petri" erwähnt.
Durch die malerischen Burkheimer Gassen
schreitet wie vor Jahrhunderten um 22 Uhr
der Nachtwächter und singt sein Lied in ale-
mannischer Sprache.

FAR BELOW BURKHEIM, our gaze wanders
to the heights of the Kaiserstuhl. The parish
church, which came into being over the
course of the centuries, was first noted in
the year 1000 as "Basilica S. Petri". Through
the picturesque streets of Burkheim march-
es the night watchman at 10 in the evening,
as in centuries gone by, and he sings his
song in the Alemannic language.

◄◄ Das Winzerdorf Achkarren beherbergt im Gebäude der historischen Zehntscheuer das Kaiserstühler Weinbaumuseum. Die Bahnstation von Achkarren liegt an der Kaiserstuhlbahn, einer der landschaftlich schönsten Bahnlinien Deutschlands. Zwischen Riegel und Breisach verkehrt auch die Museumsbahn „Rebenbummler".

The vineyard village of Achkarren houses the Kaiserstuhl Wine-Growing Museum in the building of the historical Tithe Barn. The Achkarren railway station lies on the Kaiserstuhl Railway, a railway line with some of the most beautiful scenery in Germany. The museum railway "Rebenbummler" also runs on this line, between Riegel and Breisach.

◄ Vogtsburg im Kaiserstuhl ist die größte Weinbaugemeinde Baden-Württembergs. Sie besteht aus sieben malerisch gelegenen Winzerorten im zentralen und im westlichen Kaiserstuhl, darunter Burkheim, Achkarren, Ihringen (oben) und Bischoffingen (unten), Hauptort ist Oberrotweil (Mitte). In der gotischen Friedhofskirche St. Michael in Niederrotweil befindet sich ein spätgotischer Schnitzaltar (um 1525). Mit einem Viertel der badischen Rebfläche bilden die vulkanischen Hänge des Kaiserstuhls das größte Weinbaugebiet Badens.

Vogtsburg in Kaiserstuhl is the largest wine-growing community in Baden-Württemberg. It is comprised of seven picturesquely located vineyard-towns in central and western Kaiserstuhl, with Burkheim, Achkarren, Ihringen (top) and Bischoffingen (bottom) among these; the main town is Oberrotweil (middle). In the Gothic cemetery church St. Michael in Niederrotweil, a Gothic carved altar is found (around 1525). With one-quarter of the Badish vineyard-acreage, the volcanic slopes of the Kaiserstuhl form the largest wine growing-area of Baden.

◄ OBERBERGEN liegt im Herzen des Kaiserstuhls zwischen den Rebhängen der Weinlage Baßgeige (Aufnahmestandort) und dem Totenkopf. Der Neunlindenbuck (556 m) mit einem Aussichtsturm und der Totenkopf (557 m) mit dem Sendeturm bilden als Doppelgipfel die höchste Erhebung des Kaiserstuhls, der sich als kleines vulkanisches Mittelgebirge zwischen Freiburg und Colmar aus der Oberrheinebene erhebt. Während die Hochlagen von Vogesen und Schwarzwald bis weit ins Frühjahr hinein verschneit, vereist oder von der Schneeschmelze betroffen sind, ist der sonnige Kaiserstuhl mit seinem extrem milden Klima – das Winzerdorf Ihringen an seinem Südfuß ist der wärmste Ort Deutschlands – meist schon im März schneefrei und ideal geeignet für Wanderungen im Spätwinter und zeitigen Frühjahr. Die Kammwanderung auf dem sichelförmigen Kaiserstuhl-Vulkankrater führt in alten Laubwäldern und Hochweiden mit traumhaften Aufblicken zu den Bergen von Schwarzwald und Vogesen zur Wallfahrtskapelle auf dem Katharinenberg und zum Neunlinden-Aussichtsturm.

◄ OBERBERGEN lies in the heart of the Kaiserstuhl, between the vineyard-slopes of the wine location Baßgeige (photo location) and Totenkopf, topped by a transmitter tower. The Neunlindenbuck (556 m) with look-out tower and the Totenkopf (557 m) with transmitter tower form a double peak of the highest points of Kaiserstuhl's elevation, rising up from the Upper Rhine between Freiburg and Colmar as a volcanic island mountain. While the plateaus of Vogesen and the Black Forest are snowy, icy and affected by the thawing period well into the springtime, the sunny Kaiserstuhl mountain country, with its extremely mild climate – the vineyard village Ihringen on its southern foot is the warmest location in Germany – is usually snow-free by March and a paradise for hiking in late winter and early spring. The hike along the ridge of the sickle-shaped Kaiserstuhl volcano crater leads through old deciduous woodland and high pastures, with a fantastic view out on the mountains of the Black Forest and Vogesen, to the pilgrimage chapel on the Katharinenberg and to the Neunlinden look-out tower.

▶ **SANKT TRUDPERT** im Münstertal ist die älteste Niederlassung der Benediktiner im Schwarzwald. In malerischer Lage schmiegen sich die vom Barockbaumeister Peter Thumb 1738–49 errichteten Gebäude in den Wiesenhang zu Füßen des Belchenmassivs. 1806, während der napoleonischen Kriege wurde das Kloster aufgehoben. Seit 1920 befindet sich die Anlage im Besitz einer nach benediktinischen Regeln lebenden Schwesterngemeinschaft. Die Gästetrakte stehen allen offen, die zur Ruhe kommen, Kraft schöpfen, zu sich selbst und zu Gott finden wollen. Benannt ist das Kloster nach dem irisch-schottischen Benediktiner Trudpert, der im Jahr 604 aus dem Elsass ins Münstertal wanderte und auf einem Hügel in der Wildnis die erste Einsiedelei gründete. Nach nur drei Jahren wurde er erschlagen; die Sankt-Trudpert-Kapelle des Klosters wurde 1698/1700 über der legendären Mordstätte errichtet. – Die Feldprozession (unten) folgt dem Wanderweg vom Kloster Richtung Belchen.

SAINT TRUDPERT in the Münster Valley is the oldest Benedictine location in the Black Forest. In a picturesque location, the buildings erected by the baroque master builder Peter Thumb between 1738 and 1749, at the meadow bank at the foot of the Belchen Mountain. During the Napoleonic Wars, the monastery was closed in 1806. Since 1920, the facilities are owned by a community of nuns, living according to Benedictine rules. The guest wing is open to all who seek peace and quiet, who wish to gather their strength, to find themselves and God. The monastery is named after the Iro-Scottish Benedictine Trudpert, who emigrated in the year 604 from the Alsace to the Münster Valley and established upon a hill in the wilderness the first hermitage. After only three years, he was slain; a chapel was built in 1698/1700 upon the legendary site of the murder. – The field procession (below) follows the hiking path from the monastery in the direction of Belchen.

► DAS WASSERSCHLOSS ENTENSTEIN in Schliengen zählt zu den Perlen des Markgräflerlands. Der Barockbau mit zugehörigem Landschaftspark ging aus einem von Wasser umgebenen mittelalterlichen Wohnturm hervor und fungiert heute als Rathaus. Die in der Vorbergzone des Südschwarzwalds gelegenen Teile des Markgräflerlands sind ein bedeutendes Weinanbaugebiet, das Foto unten links zeigt die Weinlese. Markgraf Karl Friedrich von Baden ließ 1780 Gutedelreben (Chasselas) aus Vevey am Genfer See einführen; auf 40 Prozent der 3000 Hektar umfassenden Ertragsrebfläche wird heute Gutedel angebaut. Ebringen (oben rechts) am Westhang des Schönbergs ist der früheste urkundlich erwähnte Weinbauort im Breisgau. Von der Kapelle auf dem Ehrenstetter Ölberg (unten rechts) schweift der Blick über das Hexental hinweg bis zum Belchen.

► THE "WASSERSCHLOSS" (Water Castle) Entenstein in Schliengen numbers among the treasures of the Markgräflerland. The baroque structure, surrounded by a scenic park, originated from a medieval residential tower, serving today as town hall. This part of the Markgräflerland, lying in the foothills of the southern Black Forest, is an important wine-growing region; the photo on the lower left shows a grape harvest. In 1780, Margrave Karl Friedrich of Baden had white grape vines (Chasselas) imported from Vevey on Lake Geneva; today Chasselas is cultivated on 40 % of the 3000 hectare comprising the land under vines. Ebringen (upper right) in the western slope of the Schönberg is the earliest documented wine-growing location in Breisgau. From the chapel on the Ehrenstetten Ölberg (lower right) our gaze wanders across the Hexen Valley all the way to the Belchen mountain.

◄ **DER BELCHEN** ist die imposanteste Berggestalt des Schwarzwalds. Nach dem Feldberg und dem Herzogenhorn ist er der dritthöchste Berg (1414 m), gleichwohl gilt er als „König des Schwarzwalds". Seine unter Naturschutz stehenden Bergwiesen bieten eine überragende Aussicht auf weite Teile des Süd- und Hochschwarzwalds, auf die Rheinebene mit dem Kaiserstuhl und zu den Bergen im deutsch-französisch-schweizerischen Dreiländereck. Bei klarer Sicht und winterlichen Inversionslagen schweift der Blick von den Höhen des Südschwarzwalds über den Jura hinweg bis zu den Alpen (Mitte rechts). Ein ähnlich exzellentes Panorama wie der Belchen bietet der Kandel, der zudem ein beliebter Paragliding-Startpunkt ist (unten rechts). Die Ausgangspunkte der Wanderwege auf die hohen Berge sind oftmals selbst Idyllen wie Wieden (oben rechts) am Belchen oder der Wintersportort Hinterzarten – hier im abendlichen Lichterglanz (unten links).

THE BELCHEN is the most formidable mountainous form of the Black Forest. Following the Feldberg and the Herzogenhorn, it is the third largest mountain (1414 m), and at the same time considered "King of the Black Forest". Protected under nature conservation, its mountain meadows provide an outstanding view of extensive parts of the southern and upper Black Forest, of the Rhine plain with the Kaiserstuhl and to the mountains in the tri-border region of France–Switzerland–Germany. With a clear view and inverted winter conditions, our view wanders from the high mountains of the Black Forest across Jura and beyond to the Alps (middle right). A similarly excellent panoramic view as Belchen is offered by the Kandel, which is also a favourite paragliding starting point (lower right). The starting points for the hiking trails on the high mountains are often idyllic spots, like Wieden (upper right) on Belchen or the winter-sports town of Hinterzarten – seen here in the glow of evening light (below left).

▶ **WALDSHUT** war bis 1801 die wichtigste der vier vorderösterreichischen Waldstädte und hat sein attraktives Altstadtbild bis heute bewahrt. Unteres Tor (oben) und Oberes Tor (unten) und zahlreiche weitere Bauten bilden ein ungewöhnlich geschlossenes historisches Ensemble.

WALDSHUT was the most important of the four Anterior Austrian forest cities on the Upper Rhine up until 1801, and it has preserved its lovely old city character. Lower (above) and Upper Gate (below) and numerous other structures form a historical ensemble of incredible unity.

▶▶ **BAD SÄCKINGEN** wartet in der Altstadt mit dem monumentalen Fridolinsmünster auf. Zwischen dem deutschen und dem schweizerischen Hochrheinufer spannt sich auf Steinpfeilern die mit 203,7 Metern längste gedeckte Holzbrücke Europas.

THE MONUMENTAL FRIDOLIN MINSTER awaits in Bad Säckingen's old city center. Between the German and Swiss banks of the Upper Rhine, spanning across 203.7 meters on stone pillars, is Europe's longest roofed wooden bridge.

▶▶ **LAUFENBURG** an der schmalsten Stelle des Hochrheins ist seit den napoleonischen Kriegen geteilt: Rechtsrheinisch liegt der kleinere badische (im Bild), linksrheinisch im Kanton Aargau der schweizerische Teil. Seinen Namen verdankt der Ort den „Louffen", Stromschnellen, die bis 1914 durch den zwölf Meter schmalen Hochrhein-Canyon tosten.

LAUFENBURG, on the narrowest point of the Upper Rhine, is a divided city since the Napoleonic Wars: To the right of the Rhine lies the smaller Badish half (pictured), and left of the Rhine, in the Swiss canton of Aargau, the main city of the district Laufenburg. Laufenburg's name goes back to the rapids called "Louffen," which up until 1914 roared through the then only 12 meter wide Upper Rhine canyon.

◄◄ **Der Schluchsee** ist der größte Schwarzwaldsee und ein Wassersportparadies für Segler und Surfer. Seine nahezu unverbaute Uferlinie macht ihn zu einem Dorado für Wanderer und Radwanderer.
The Schluchsee is the largest lake in the Black Forest and a water sports paradise for sailing and surfing. Its nearly completely undeveloped shoreline makes it an El Dorado for hikers and cyclists.

◄◄ **Das Bernauer Hochtal** liegt auf gut 900 Metern Höhe zwischen Blößling, Spießhorn und Schnepfhalde. Der erste Mönch des Klosters St. Blasien soll „Bernova" geheißen haben und so namengebend für Bernau gewesen sein.
The Bernauer Hochtal Valley lies at a good height of 900 meter between Blößling, Spießhorn and Schnepfhalde. The first monk of Saint Blasien is said to have been named "Bernova," from which the name "Bernau" is derived.

◄ **Sankt Blasien** ist ein heilklimatischer Kurort im oberen Albtal. Die Vierflügelanlage der ehemaligen Benediktinerabtei prägt das Ortsbild. Heute beherbergen die Gebäude das Kolleg, ein von Jesuiten geleitetes Internat. Die Kuppel des Doms (1783) ist nach der des Pariser Panthéons und der der Peterskirche in Rom die drittgrößte der Erde (Mitte). Tritt man aus der Kollegspforte, gelangt man in den Kurpark (unten), hinter dem die Alb rauscht (oben).
Saint Blasien is a popular climatic health resort in upper Alb Valley. The character of the town has been shaped by the complex of the four-winged former Benedictine abbey. Today, the buildings house a boarding school lead by Jesuits. The dome of the cathedral (1783) is, following the Panthéon in Paris and Peter's Church in Rome, the third largest in the world (middle). When exiting the gates of the college, one can reach the spa park (below), and beyond that rushes the Alb (above).

▶ **DIE WUTACHSCHLUCHT** ist der eindrucksvollste Canyon des Schwarzwalds, nahezu die gesamte Schlucht steht unter Naturschutz einschließlich der Lotenbachklamm (rechts) und weiterer Seitentäler. Die Wanderung durch die Wutachschlucht ist eine Zeitreise durch 100 Millionen Jahre Erdgeschichte. Wie in einem geologischen Lehrbuch schneidet die Wutach fast alle Gesteinsschichten Südwestdeutschlands an, der Europäische Fernwanderweg 1 und der Querweg Freiburg–Bodensee führen von Lenzkirch-Kappel auf einer Länge von elf Kilometern durch den Gneis- und Granitabschnitt der Schlucht zur Gaststätte „Schattenmühle", es folgen zwölf Kilometer im Muschelkalk- und Keuperabschnitt bis zur Wutachmühle. Die Wutach hat sich in den Muschelkalk derart tief eingegraben, dass Fluss und Pfad über weite Strecken von nahezu senkrechten Felswänden flankiert werden.

THE WUTACH CANYON is the most impressive Black Forest canyon, and nearly the entire section of the canyon valley is subject to nature preservation, including the Lotenbachklamm (right) and further valleys. Hiking through the Wutach Canyon is a travel back in time through 100 million years of the earth history, and like a geological textbook, the Wutach cuts through nearly all the layers of rock in southwestern Germany; the European long-distance hiking trail 1 and the crossing path Freiburg–Lake Constance lead from Lenzkirch-Kappel at a distance of 11 kilometers through the gneiss and granite sections of the canyon to the "Schattenmühle" restaurant, followed by 12 kilometers in the shell limestone and keuper sections up to the Wutachmühle. The Wutach has penetrated into the shell limestone in such a way that the river and the path are flanked by vertical cliff walls over long sections of the route, running with passageways secured by railings and other safety fixtures.

► SAIG zwischen Titisee und Hochfirst ist der höchstgelegene Ortsteil der Gemeinde Lenzkirch, seine Tradition als ruhiger, naturnaher Kurort reicht bis ins 19. Jahrhundert zurück. Die gotische Kirche und die wenigen Häuser liegen in den Wiesen des Hochfirst-Südhangs mit Blick auf die höchsten Schwarzwaldberge. Originelle Wegweiser zeigen im Dorf die Richtung an.

SAIG, between Lake Titisee and Hochfirst, is the highest lying part of the Lenzkirch municipalty, with its tradition as a peaceful, natural health resort dating back to the 19th century. The Gothic church and small scattering of houses are found in the meadow of the Hochfirst—south slope, with a view of the highest Black Forest mountains. Original hiking route signs in the village indicate the direction.

►► DER TITISEE ist der größte Natursee des Schwarzwalds und dank der Aussicht bis zum Feldberggipfel sowie für Wassersportler, Wanderer und Radfahrer zu jeder Jahreszeit ein Traumziel. Der im Feldseekar entspringende Seebach speist mit seinem kristallklaren Wasser den zwischen bewaldete Berghänge eingebetteten eiszeitlichen Moränenstausee. Der Ausfluss des Titisees ist die Gutach, die sich wenige Kilometer unterhalb mit der Haslach zur Wutach vereinigt und den großartigsten Canyon des Schwarzwalds ausgewaschen hat.

THE TITISEE is the largest natural lake in the Black Forest, and thanks to the view reaching out to the summit of the Feldberg, as well as the possibilities offered for water sports, hiking and cycling, it is a favorite destination all year round. The Seebach, originating in Feldseekar, feeds with its crystal clear mountain water the ice-age lake, embedded between wooded slopes; the outlet of Lake Titisee is the Gutach, which unites a few kilometres below with the Haslach into the Wutach, and forming the most spectaculat canyon of the Black Forest.

◄◄ LANDSCHAFTLICHE SCHÖNHEIT und Abwechslungsreichtum haben den Südschwarzwald zur beliebtesten Wanderregion der deutschen Mittelgebirge werden lassen – Gipfel und mattenbedeckte Kammfluren mit herrlicher Aussicht, Seen, Moore und Schluchten. Dank der hervorragenden Infrastruktur ist der Südschwarzwald ein Wandergebiet für alle Ansprüche. Kein Wunder also, dass schon im Jahr 1864 in Freiburg mit dem Schwarzwaldverein der älteste deutsche Gebirgs- und Wanderverein gegründet wurde. Zahlreich sind an den Wanderwegen auch die alten, oft liebevoll geschnitzten Markierungsschilder (oben rechts). Die Holzverarbeitung ist traditionell ein wichtiges Gewerbe im Südschwarzwald, das Foto in der Mitte zeigt die Sägemühle des Weberhansenhofs bei Hinterzarten.

ITS BEAUTIFUL LANDSCAPE and great variety have made the southern Black Forest into the most beloved hiking regions of the Central German Uplands – the summit and alpine meadows, lakes, marshland and canyons. Thanks to the excellent infrastructure the southern Black Forest hiking area meets every need. So it is no wonder, that already in the year 1864 the "Schwarzwaldverein" was founded in Freiburg as the oldest German mountain and hiking association. There are still many of the old, lovingly carved, wooden signs marking the trails (upper right). Woodworking is traditionally an important trade in the Black Forest, and the photo in the middle depicts a sawmill of the Weberhansenhof near Hinterzarten.

◄ DER GOLFSPORT findet im Schwarzwald immer mehr Zuspruch. Im Bild das Gelände des Golfklubs Hochschwarzwald zwischen Titisee und Hinterzarten.

GOLFING contines to enjoy ever-increasing popularity in the Black Forest. Pictured is the land of the Hochschwarzwald golf club between Titisee and Hinterzarten.

DER MITTLERE SCHWARZWALD reicht natur-
räumlich vom Dreisam- und vom Höllental nordwärts bis zur Wasserscheide zwischen Kinzig und Rench sowie bis zum
Kniebis an der Wasserscheide von Kinzig
und Murg. Die zentrale Landschaft ist die
Ortenau, die bedeutendsten Flüsse sind
Kinzig und Elz, größte Stadt ist Offenburg,
die Kreisstadt des Ortenaukreises. Vom
Dreisamtal bei Freiburg bis zur Südgrenze
der Ortenau liegt dieses Gebiet im Naturpark Südschwarzwald, der ungeachtet dieses Namens weite Teile des mittleren
Schwarzwalds umfasst. Der Rosskopf
(Foto) auf dem alten „Dreiländereck" zwischen Dreisam- und Wildtal ist der ge-
meinsame Hausberg von Freiburg, Ebnet
und Gundelfingen mit prachtvollem Blick
auf den Süd- und den mittleren Schwarzwald sowie über den Kaiserstuhl hinweg
bis zu den Vogesen.

THE MIDDLE BLACK FOREST'S natural
boundaries range from the Dreisam Valley
and Höllen Valley northward up to the
water divide between Kinzig and Rench, as
well as to Kniebis on the water divide of
Kinzig and Murg. Central to the landscape
is Ortenau, the most important rivers are
Kinzig and Elz, the largest city is Offenburg, the chief town of the Ortenau district. From the Dreisam Valley near
Freiburg up to the south border of the
Ortenau, this area lies in the area of nature
preserve South Black Forest, which despite
its name encompasses wide areas of the
central Black Forest. The Rosskopf (photo)
at the old "Dreiländereck" (three-border
point) between the Dreisam and Wild Valleys, the shared mountain of Freiburg,
Ebnet and Gundelfingen, with an exquisite
view upon the southern and central Black
Forest, as well as beyond the Kaiserstuhl
out to the Vogesen.

▶ **DIE GRÖSSTE KUCKUCKSUHR** ist in Schonachbach zu bewundern, sie misst 4,5 mal 4,5 Meter und wiegt 6 Tonnen. Im Dorf Waldau bei Sankt Märgen sollen im 17. Jahrhundert die ersten Schwarzwalduhren gefertigt worden sein, um 1730 versah die Uhrmacherfamilie Ketterer im Baslertal in Schönwald die Uhren erstmals mit einem Kuckuck. Am „Höfle" erinnert ein Gedenkstein an diese Erfindung.

THE LARGEST CUCKOO-CLOCK, measuring 4.50 x 4.50 meter and having a total weight of 6 tons, may be seen in Schonachbach. In the village of Waldau near Saint Märgen, the first Black Forests clocks are said to have been manufactured in the 17th century, and around 1730 the clock-making family Ketterer im Basler Valley in Schönwald fitted a clock for the first time with a cuckoo. On the "Höfle" a stone-marker memorializes the invention.

▶ **DER VOGTSBAUERNHOF** ist das meistbesuchte Freilichtmuseum des Schwarzwalds. Es präsentiert Schwarzwaldhäuser mit Originaleinrichtung. Umfangreich ist auch das Rahmenprogramm mit Sonderausstellungen, Vorführungen der Mühlen, Sägen und handwerklichen Tätigkeiten.

THE VOGTSBAUERNHOF is the most frequently visited open-air museum in the Black Forest. It presents Black Forest houses with original furnishings. Its program is wide ranging, with its special exhibitions and presentations of the mills, sawmills and handicraft activities.

▶▶ **DIE RAINBAUERNMÜHLE** am Ottenhöfener Mühlenweg im Achertal. Neun Getreidemühlen und eine Hammerschmiede sind an diesem Rundwanderweg zu sehen.

THE RAINBAUERN MILL on the Ottenhöfener Mühlenweg in the Acher Valley. Nine grain mills and a blacksmith may by seen on this circular hiking route.

▼ „DER SCHUTTIG IST LOS" heißt es bei der Elzacher Fasnet (oben links und rechts). Hauptfigur der dreitägigen Fastnacht ist der Schuttig, eine archaische Gestalt mit rotem Zottelgewand, Schneckenhut mit Wollbollen und Holzlarve. Die Hauptfigur der Villinger Fasnet ist der „Narro" (unten links): Er gilt als der Aristokrat der alemannischen Fastnacht.

▶▶ BURG HORNBERG ist die Ruine der um 1200 errichteten Burg der Herren von Hornberg. Sie thront auf dem Schlossberg hoch über dem Gutachtal. Im Vordergrund der Pulverturm, dahinter der Bergfried. Das Hornberger Schießen ist ein mündlich überlieferter Schildbürgerstreich, der sich um 1564 zugetragen haben soll und heute als historisches Spiel auf der Freilichtbühne von Hornberg aufgeführt wird. Der Hornberger Ortsteil Reichenbach ist die Heimat der Schwarzwälder Bollenhuttracht (unten rechts).

▼ "DER SCHUTTIG IST LOS"(It's Schuttig time), the season of the fire-ritual during the Elzach Fasnet carnival (above left and right). The main character of the three-day Fasnet is the Schuttig, an archaic figure with red shaggy clothing, fool's cap with woollen balls and wooden mask. The main character of the Villingen Fasnet is the "Narro" (lower left): The Narro is considered the aristocrat of the Alemannic carnival.

▶ HORNBERG CASTLE is the ruins of the fortress constructed by the Lord of Hornberg at around the year 1200. It stands upon the Schlossberg high above the Gutach valley. The "Hornberger Schießen" concerns a piece of bungling, said to have originated around 1564, and which is today a stage play performed on the open-air stage of Hornberg. The Hornberg district of Reichenbach is the home of the traditional Black Forest "Bollenhut" (lower right).

◄ SCHILTACH ist eine alte Schiffer- und Holzhandelsstadt im Kinzigtal mit denkmalgeschützter Altstadt an der Deutschen Fachwerkstraße. Den Marktplatz (oben rechts) im Herzen der Altstadt konzipierte der in Herrenberg geborene Renaissancebaumeister Heinrich Schickhardt nach dem Stadtbrand von 1590. Der Platz um den Marktbrunnen ist seither Schauplatz traditioneller Märkte und Feste. Das Museum am Markt dokumentiert die Geschichte dieses Bilderbuch-Städtchens, dessen neoromanische Kirche zwischen 1838 und 1842 erbaut wurde (oben links). Als Schiltach Ende des 19. Jahrhunderts Eisenbahn- und Straßenknotenpunkt wurde, endete mit der letzten Floßfahrt 1894 auch die traditionsreiche Schifferei.

SCHILTACH is an old marine and lumber mercantile city in Kinzig Valley, with an old city center under heritage protection, located on the Deutschen Fachwerkstraße. The market place (upper right) in the heart of the old city center was conceived by the Renaissance architect Heinrich Schickhardt, following the city fire of 1590. Since that time, the square surrounding the market fountain is the site of historical markets and festivals. The museum on the marketplace documents the history of this picture-book city, whose neo-romanesque church was built between 1838 and 1842 (upper left). When Schiltach became the juncture of streets and railways at the end of the 19th century, the long tradition of water travel ended with the final raft ride in 1894.

◀ **ALPIRSBACH** im Kinzigtal hat mit dem ehemaligen Benediktinerkloster ein bedeutendes Zeugnis kluniazensischer Reformarchitektur bewahrt. Die außen schmucklose, in rotem Buntsandstein errichtete romanische Säulenbasilika zählt zu den wenigen unversehrt erhaltenen Schöpfungen der Hirsauer Bauschule. Im spätgotischen Kreuzgang (unten) finden seit 1952 die sommerlichen „Kreuzgangkonzerte" statt. Gegründet wurde das Kloster 1095 von reformorientierten Benediktinern aus dem Südschwarzwaldkloster Sankt Blasien. Der Einfluss der Hirsauer Reform spiegelt sich in der Architektur der um 1130 vollendeten Klosterkirche. Das Besondere der Hirsauer Reform war, dass sie sich auf die Grundlagen des abendländischen Mönchtums nach der Benediktregel besann: Bete und arbeite („ora et labora"), Besitzlosigkeit, strikte Beachtung der Liturgie, soziale Verantwortung. Ein Zehntel der Einkünfte floss in Sozialfonds, mit denen Armenhäuser und andere Einrichtungen für Bedürftige finanziert wurden. Die Reduktion auf das Wesentliche sollte sich auch in der Architektur äußern.

◀ **ALPIRSBACH** in the Kinzig Valley has, with the former Benedictine monastery, preserved an important testament to the cluniazensic reform period architecture. The Romanesque column basilica, made of red sandstone, with its ornament-free exterior, is among the few preserved works of the Hirsau school of architecture. Since 1952, the late-Gothic cloister (below) serves as the stage of the summer "Kreuzgangkonzerte" (cloister concerts). The monastery was established in 1095 by reformed Benedictines from the South Black Forest monastery Saint Blasien. The influence of the Hirsau Reform is reflected in the architecture of the monastery church, completed around 1130. What is special about the Hirsau Reform, is that it was based upon the rules governing the Benedictines as it affected Western monks: Prayer and labor ("ora et labora"), poverty, faithful adherence to the liturgy, social responsibility. One-tenth of the revenue was channelled into a social fund, with poorhouses, and other facilities for the needy was financed. A reduction to the essentials was also to be expressed in the architecture.

◄◄ OFFENBURG ist die Hauptstadt der Ortenau. Die Messe- und Medienstadt am Austritt der Kinzig aus dem mittleren Schwarzwald ist eine Gründung der Zähringer (um 1100), der Stauferkaiser Friedrich II. erhob sie 1204 zur Reichsstadt. Zu den Repräsentativbauten der Barockzeit zählen das Rathaus (oben links), das Haus der Ortenauer Ritterschaft und die Landvogtei. Schloss Staufenberg (unten links) hoch über dem Winzerort Durbach (unten rechts: das Winzerhaus von Durbach) ging aus einer der zahlreichen mittelalterlichen Höhenburgen bei Offenburg hervor. Die Markgrafen von Baden ließen die alten Gemäuer im 19. Jahrhundert zum Schloss umbauen und erweitern und unterhalten hier ein Weingut mit der Lage „Schloss Staufenberg". Das im neugotischen Stil an der Stelle einer mittelalterlichen staufischen Reichsburg errichtete Schloss Ortenberg (oben rechts) ist ebenfalls eine durch die Romantik inspririerte Nachschöpfung.

OFFENBURG is the capital of Ortenau. The trade fair and media city at the river Kinzig was founded by the House of Zähringen (around 1100), the emperor Friedrich II of Hohenstaufen declared it an imperial city in 1204. The Town Hall (above left) is among the representative structures from the baroque period, as are the house of the Ortenau Knighthood and the Landvogtei (House of Governership). Staufenberg Castle (below left), high above the vineyard town of Durbach (below right: the vineyard house of Durbach), arose from one of the many medieval hilltop fortresses near Offenburg. The Margrave of Baden has the old masonry rebuild and extended as a castle in the 19th century, and maintained a vineyard here called "Schloss Staufenberg." The neo gothic style replacing the medieval Hohenstaufen fortress as the Ortenberg Castle (upper right) is also a work created in the spirit of the Romantic period.

◄◄ GENGENBACH, im Kinzigtal gelegen, lockt schon von ferne mit der Sieben-Türme-Silhouette der denkmalgeschützten Altstadt, alles überragt von der weithin sichtbaren Jakobskapelle auf dem „Bergle", dem Wahrzeichen der ehemaligen Reichsstadt. Stadtmauer, Wehrgang, drei Stadttore, die beiden Kirchen und eine Fülle von Fachwerkhäusern aus dem 18./19. Jahrhundert prägen die Bebauung innerhalb des mittelalterlichen Mauergürtels. Berühmt für ihre geschlossene Fachwerkbebauung ist die Engelgasse (links). Die Straßen der Altstadt laufen trichterförmig auf den Obertorturm zu (alle Fotos rechts), vor dem im Wechsel der Jahreszeiten auch die verschiedensten Feste stattfinden: Fastnacht (Fasend), Palmweihe, Fronleichnam, Weinfeste, Adventskalenderhaus, Weihnachtsmarkt (rechts unten).
GENGENBACH in Kinzigtal even attracts from afar, with the seven-tower silhouette of the heritage protected old city center, presided over by the widely visible Jakobskapelle upon the "Bergle", the symbol of the former imperial city. City wall, defensive corridor, three city gates, both churches, and a multitude of half-timbered houses from the 18th/19th centuries, influence the construction within the belt of the medieval wall. Known for its uniform half-timbered construction is the Engelgasse (left). The streets of the old city center run in a funnel-like manner toward the Upper Gate Tower (all photos to the right), which experience a variety of festivals over the course of the year: Fastnacht (Fasend), Palm Sunday, Corpus Christi, wine festivals, Advent Calendar House, Christmas market (below right).

DER NORDSCHWARZWALD ist das Heilbäderparadies des Schwarzwalds: Baden-Baden, Bad Wildbad, Bad Liebenzell, Bad Herrenalb, Waldbronn, Bad Ripoldsau-Schapbach – zahlreich sind die seit der Antike oder dem Mittelalter erschlossenen Bäder. Die Schwarzwald-Bäderstraße verbindet als 270 Kilometer langer Wellnessrundkurs die Heilbäder zwischen der „Goldstadt" Pforzheim im Norden und Freudenstadt am Kniebis im Süden. Der in der Hornisgrinde (1163 m, im Bild zu sehen: der Berg mit dem Sendeturm) gipfelnde Grindenkamm und der im Südosten anschließende Kniebis bilden den First des Nordschwarzwalds. Ihm folgen die drei bedeutendsten touristischen Leitlinien: Schwarzwaldhochstraße, Westweg und Schwarzwald-Radweg. Der breite, vermoorte Buntsandsteinkamm bildet die Wasserscheide zwischen Acher und Rench auf der Ortenauseite sowie der Murg auf der schwäbischen Seite.

THE NORTH BLACK FOREST is the health spa paradise of the Black Forest: Baden-Baden, Bad Wildbad, Bad Liebenzell, Bad Herrenalb, Waldbronn, Bad Ripoldsau-Schapbach – numerous baths were developed in antiquity or during the Middle Ages. The Schwarzwald-Bäderstraße connects, in a 270 kilometer-long health round trip, the health spas from the "Golden City" of Pforzheim in the north and Freudenstadt on the Kniebis in the south. In the Hornisgrinde (1163 m, photo: the mountain with the radio tower) peaking Grindenkamm, and the Kniebis that joins it in the southeast, form the crest of the North Black Forest. Following this are there the most important guides for tourists: Schwarzwaldhochstraße, Westweg and Schwarzwald-Radweg (Black Forest Bicycle Trail). The broad, marshy, mottled sandstone ridge forms the water divide between the Acher and Rench on the Ortenau side, as well as the Murg on the Swabian side.

▶▶ Der Mummelsee an der Südflanke der Hornisgrinde ist der tiefste Karsee des Schwarzwalds – und nach Meinung vieler der schönste. Wegen seiner Lage an der Schwarzwaldhochstraße und wegen der oft überfüllten Parkplätze und den vielen touristischen Angeboten wird er zuweilen despektierlich als „Rummelsee" bezeichnet, doch seiner Schönheit tut das keinen Abbruch. Am Berghotel (mit Restaurant: oben links) beginnt der Rundwanderweg um den See, in dessen Tiefe den Sagen zufolge Nixen, Zwerge und andere als „Mummeln" bezeichnete Wesen hausen und bei Vollmond Reigen auf den Wellen tanzen.

The Mummelsee in south slope of the Hornisgrinde is the deepest cirque lake of the Black Forest – and many consider it the most beautiful. Due to its location on the Schwarzwaldhochstraße, and because of the often overfilled large parking lot, it is sometimes disrespectfully referred to as "Lake Racket," but not even that can spoil its beauty. The round-trip hiking trail starts at the mountain hotel, leading around this lake, in the depths of which dwell, according to sagas, mermaids, dwarfs, and other fantastic creatures described as "Mummeln," which at full moon perform a round dance upon the waves.

▶ Sasbachwalden ist ein heilklimatischer und Kneippkurort mit hervorragend erhaltenem Fachwerkortskern am Westfuß der Hornisgrinde im milden Wein- und Obstbaumklima der Ortenau (unten). An der Kirche in der Ortsmitte (Mitte) beginnt der Wasserfall-Wanderweg, der in die Gaishöllschlucht führt.

Sasbachwalden is the climatic and Kneipp health resort, with a beautifully preserved half-timbered city center, located at the west foot of the Hornisgrinde in the mild vine and fruit-tree climate of Ortenau (below). Beginning at the church in the center of town (middle) is the waterfall hiking trail in the Gaishöll Canyon.

◄◄ DER FREUDENSTÄDTER MARKTPLATZ ist mit einer Fläche von 216 mal 219 Metern der größte in Deutschland. Seine Wasserfontänen und Arkaden bilden den Mittelpunkt der als „Idealstadt" der Renaissance konzipierten Residenz (1599) eines Staates, der neben dem Herzogtum Württemberg die Reichsgrafschaft Mömpelgard (Montbéliard) in Burgund umfasste. Bei der Grundsteinlegung der Stadtkirche an der Südecke des Marktplatzes erhielt die Stadt ihren Namen. Nach dem Tod Herzog Friedrichs I. von Württemberg 1608 endete der Traum von der „Freudenstadt" als Residenz – die Schönheit der Stadt ist geblieben.

THE FREUDENSTADT MARKETPLACE, with its area of 216 x 219 meters, is the largest in Germany. Its water fountains and surrounding arcades form the center of what was conceives as the Renaissance "ideal city" Residence (1599) of a state, which comprise, in addition to the Dutchy of Württemberg, the Imperial Shire of Mömpelgard (Montbéliard) in Burgund. With the laying of the groundstone of the city church, the city obtained its name: Freudenstadt (City of Joy). After the death of Duke Friedrich I of Württemberg in 1608, the dream of the "Freudenstadt" came to an end – the beauty of the city remains.

◄ ORTSIDYLLEN begeistern allenthalben im Nordschwarzwald. Baiersbronn (oben) ist heilklimatischer Kurort im oberen Murgtal, Bad Peterstal-Griesbach (Mitte) liegt im Renchtal. Dornstetten (unten) an der Deutschen Fachwerkstraße wartet mit einem sanierten Altstadtkern innerhalb der mittelalterlichen Wehrmauern auf.

IDYLLIC TOWNS bring excitement everywhere in the North Black Forest. Baiersbronn (above) is the climatic health resort of upper Murgtal, Bad Peterstal-Griesbach (middle) lies in Rench Valley. Dornstetten (below) awaits with a wonderfully restored old city center within the medieval defense walls.

▼ OBERKIRCH IM RENCHTAL hat längs des Mühlbachs fast den gesamten Fachwerkbestand vom 17. bis ins 19. Jahrhundert bewahrt. In dieser schmucken „Bachanlage" siedelten Gerber, Metzger und andere Handwerker. Die Weinbaustadt Oberkirch gehörte ab 1303 zum Bistum Straßburg; während der napoleonischen Kriege kam Oberkirch 1803 an Baden. – Das Foto oben rechts zeigt das waldreiche Laufbachtal in der Gemeinde Lauf am Westfuß der Hornisgrinde.
▼ und ▶ ALTENSTEIG zeichnet sich durch seine malerische mittelalterliche Stadtanlage aus (unten links). Das Obere Schloss beherrscht das sich um den Burgberg gruppierende Mittelalterdorf Berneck bei Altensteig (rechts).
▼ DAS MÜNSTER VON SCHWARZACH bei Rastatt wurde um 1200 als Benediktinerklosterkirche errichtet unter dem Einfluss der Hirsauer Reform (unten rechts).

▼ OBERKIRCH in Rench Valley has, along the length of the Mühlbach, preserved almost all of the half-timbered structures from the 17th to 19th centuries. In this smart "Bachanlage" settled tanners, butchers and other craftsmen. The wine-growing city of Oberkirch belongs to the diocese Strasbourg since 1303; during the Napoleonic Wars, Oberkirch joined Baden in 1803. – The photo on the right shows the heavily wooded Laufbach Valley in the municipality of Lauf.
▼ and ▶ ALTENSTEIG is distiguished by its picturesque medieval city location (upper left). The Upper Castle dominates the medieval village Berneck near Altensteig, grouped around the Burgberg (Castle Mountain – right page).
▼ THE MINSTER OF SCHWARZACH near Rastatt was constructed around 1200, as a Benedictine monastery church under the influence of the Hirsau Reform (below right).

◀◀ BADEN-BADEN war unter dem Namen „Aquae" schon in der römischen Antike ein berühmtes Heilbad, seit dem 19. Jahrhundert ist die Kurstadt im Oostal Inbegriff einer kultivierten Bäderstadt mit internationalem Flair. Die Lichtentaler Allee entlang der Oos zählt zu den schönsten Landschaftsparks im Schwarzwald. Das 1824 eröffnete Kasino, in dem Tolstoi und Dostojewski („Der Spieler") die Kugel rollen ließen, ist die größte Spielbank Deutschlands und mit ihren prachtvollen Sälen im Stil französischer Königsschlösser eine der schönsten der Welt. Das Foto auf der linken Seite zeigt die Brunnenanlage am Augustusplatz, auf der rechten Seite sind oben und in der Mitte jeweils Kurhaus und Kasino zu sehen. Die klassizistische Trinkhalle neben dem Kurhaus im Oostal am Fuß des Friesenbergs wurde 1839–42 von Heinrich Hübsch errichtet, um den Gästen in stilvoller Umgebung den Genuss des Baden-Badener Heilwasser zu ermöglichen.

BADEN-BADEN was already a well-known health spa under the name "Aquae" in Roman antiquity, and since the 19th century this health resort in the Oos Valley has exemplified the cultivated spa city with international flair. The Lichtentaler Allee along the Oos is among the most beautiful landscaped parks in the Black Forest. The Casino, which opened in 1824, hosted such high rollers as Tolstoy and Dostoyevski ("The Gambler"); it is the largest of its kind in Germany, and with its grand halls in the style of the French royal castles it is one of the most beautiful in the world. The photo on the left shows the fountains on Augustusplatz, and on the right, above and in the middle respectively, the Spa and Casino. The classical Trinkhalle next to the Spa in Oostal, at the foot of the Friesenberg, was erected by Heinrich Hübsch in 1839-42, so that the guests would be able to imbibe the Baden-Baden spa water in stylish surroundings.

▶ **Prachtvolle historische Bauten**
prägen Baden-Baden, ob an der Luisenstraße (oben links), am Leopoldsplatz (rechte
Seite) oder an der Lichtentaler Allee (unten:
Theater). Die 1655 als Eichenallee von der
Stadt zum Zisterzienserinnenkloster Lich-
tental angelegte Lichtentaler Allee wurde
1850–70 zum Landschaftspark entlang der
Oos erweitert. Über 300 verschiedene ein-
heimische und exotische Bäume und Pflan-
zen säumen den Weg. Gusseiserne Stege
verbinden die Allee mit den Parks am rechten Ufer der Oos. Stadtseitiger Ausgangs-
punkt der 2300 Meter langen Allee ist der
Goetheplatz mit dem Neorenaissance-Bau
des von Charles Couteau nach dem Vorbild
der Pariser Oper errichteten Theaters;
anlässlich der Eröffnung wurde 1862 die
Oper "Béatrice und Bénédict" von Hector
Berlioz uraufgeführt.

Grand historical structures character-
ize Baden-Baden, whether on Luisenstraße
(left), on Leopoldsplatz (right side) or on
Lichtentaler Allee (below: theater). Designed in 1655 as an oak tree lane from the
city to the Cistercian Monastery of Lichten
Valley, Lichtentaler Allee was extended to
the landscaped park along the Oos in the
years 1850–70. Over 300 varieties of
domestic and exotic trees and plants line
the way. Wrought iron footbridges connect
the lane with the parks on the right bank of
the Oos. The starting point on the city side
of the 2300-meter long lane is Goetheplatz,
with the neo-Renaissance Theater designed
by Charles Couteau, modelled after the
Paris Opera; for the opening in 1862, was
the premier of the opera comique "Béatrice
and Bénédict" by Hector Berlioz.

◄◄ **DIE BADEN-BADENER STIFTSKIRCHE** auf dem Marktplatz am Florentinerberg ist das älteste Bauwerk der Altstadt und die Grablege von 14 Markgrafen, darunter das Grab Ludwig Wilhelm I., des „Türkenlouis" (1655–1707), der durch seinen Abwehrsieg bei Szlankamen das Abendland rettete. Die Stiftskirche wurde dort errichtet, wo sich ehemals die römischen Thermen befanden. Der ursprünglich romanische Bau wurde im Lauf der Jahrhunderte mehrfach erweitert.
THE BADEN-BADEN STIFTSKIRCHE (monastery church) on the marketplace on the Florentinerberg is the oldest structure of the old city center, and is the burial site of 14 margraves, among them "Türkenlouis" Ludwig Wilhelm I (1655–1707), who saved the West with his victorious defense at Szlankamen. The Stiftskirche was erected in the area of the Roman hot springs, and the originally Romanesque structure was modified several times over the centuries.

◄ **AUF DEN BATTERT-FELSEN** stehen die Ruinen des Alten Schlosses, der einstigen Hauptburg der Markgrafen von Baden. Der markgräfliche Zähringer Hermann II. ließ hier ab 1102 die Burg Hohenbaden errichten und nannte sich 1112 nach ihr „von Baden".
ON THE BATTERT FELSEN (cliffs) stand the ruins of the Altes Schloss (old castle), formerly the main fortress of the Margrave of Baden. Hermann II, the Zähringen Margrave, had the Hohenbaden fortress build here beginning in 1102, and named himself "von Baden" after it in 1112.

◄ **IN DER ROSENSTADT** Baden-Baden treffen sich im Rosenneuheitengarten auf dem Beutig alljährlich im Sommer Liebhaber, Züchter und Preisrichter, um die schönste aller Rosen zu küren.
IN THE "ROSE CITY" of Baden-Baden, flower lovers, growers and judges meet in summer each year in the "Rosenneuheitengarten" (the garden of novel roses) on the Beutig, to chose the most beautiful of all roses.

▼ SCHWARZWÄLDER KIRSCHTORTE ist die beliebteste deutsche Torte und in der gesamten westlichen Welt ein Begriff für Tortenkultur. Mancher, der beim Genuss dieser Sahnetorte ins Schwärmen gerät, denkt vielleicht an ein Schwarzwaldmädel: die Schokostreusel schwarz wie ihr Kleid, weiß wie ihre Bluse die Sahne, die Kirschen so rot wie die Bollen auf ihrem Hut. Weitere Delikatessen sind Schwarzwaldwälder Schinken und Kirschwasser, und wie am Mummelsee wird das Brot noch vielerorts aus dem Holzofen geholt.

► KUCKUCKSUHREN sind ein Exportschlager aus dem Schwarzwald. Leiter der 1850 von Großherzog Leopold von Baden in Furtwangen gegründeten staatlichen Uhrmacherschule wurde Robert Gerwig, der Erbauer der Schwarzwaldbahn. Heute beherbergt Furtwangen das Deutsche Uhrenmuseum.

▼ THE BLACK-FOREST CHERRY CAKE is the best loved German cake, and in the western world it is the epitome of the art of cake making. Some, who rhapsodize while enjoying this creamy cake, secretly think of a Black Forest girl: the sprinkled chocolate flakes as black as her dress, the cream as white as her blouse, the cherries as red as the balls on her hat. Other delicacies are Black Forest ham and kirsch, and as at Lake Mummelsee, in many places the bread is baked in wood-burning ovens.

► CUCKOO-CLOCKS are a worldwide export hit from the Black Forest. Director of the state watch-making school in Furtwangen, founded in 1850 by Grand Duke Leopold of Baden, was Robert Gerwig, the builder of the Black Forest railway. Today, Furtwangen is the home of the German Clock Museum.

▶▶ DIE PAGODENBURG im Schlosspark von Rastatt wurde 1722 als Teehaus der markgräflichen Familie errichtet. Markgraf Ludwig Wilhelm I. von Baden-Baden, der Türkenlouis, übersiedelte im Herbst 1705 aus dem von der Invasionsarmee des „Sonnenkönigs" Louis XIV. zerstörten Baden-Baden in das planmäßig als neue Residenzstadt angelegte Rastatt. Die nach dem Vorbild von Versailles vom Wiener Hofarchitekten Domenico Egidio Rossi zwischen 1697 und 1707 errichtete barocke Dreiflügelanlage des markgräflichen Schlosses (links oben) ist eines der größten Barockschlösser in Südwestdeutschland.

THE PAGODENBURG in Rastatt Castle Park was erected by the margrave's family as a teahouse in 1722. Margrave Ludwig Wilhelm I of Baden-Baden, the "Türkenlouis", moved in the autumn of 1705 from Baden-Baden, destroyed by the invading army of the "Sun king" Louis XIV, into Rastatt, the city planned as new residence. Modelled after Versailles, the Viennese court architect Domenico Egidio Rossi erected the baroque three-winged facilities of the Margrave's castle between 1697 and 1707 (above left), one of the largest baroque castles in southwest Germany.

▶ DIE YBURG ist das Wahrzeichen des Baden-Badener Reblands, im Hang des Ybergs liegt das Winzerdorf Varnhalt, durch das der Ortenauer Weinpfad von Baden-Baden nach Offenburg führt.

THE YBURG is the symbol of the wine country, and on the slope of the Yberg is found the vineyard village of Varnhalt, since the Ortenau wine trail leads from Baden-Baden to Offenburg.

▶ HOLZGEDECKTE BRÜCKE IN FORBACH im Murgtal. Die Murg mündet unterhalb von Rastatt in den Rhein.

THE WOOD-COVERED BRIDGE in Forbach in the Murg Valley. The Murg flows below Rastatt into the Rhine.

▶ **WINTERSTIMMUNG AM RUHESTEIN**, der Passhöhe an der Kreuzung der Schwarzwaldhochstraße mit der Straße von Baiersbronn im Murgtal ins Rench- und ins Achertal.

▼ **BÄDER DES NORDSCHWARZWALDS** sind unter anderem Bad Teinach (oben links), Bad Wildbad (unten links) und Bad Liebenzell (unten rechts).

▼ **SCHLOSS EBERSTEIN** ist eine prachtvolle neugotische Anlage bei Gernsbach im Murgtal (oben rechts). Der sagenumwobene „Grafensprung" unterhalb des Schlosses ist frei zugänglich. Der Überlieferung zufolge gab Graf Wolf von Eberstein auf diesem Felsen seinem Pferd die Sporen, um sich der Verfolgung durch Graf Eberhard von Württemberg zu entziehen; während das Pferd im Murgtal zerschmetterte, konnte sich Wolf von Eberstein retten. An den kühnen Ritt erinnert die Weinlage „Schloss Ebersteiner Grafensprung".

▶ **WINTER MOOD ON RUHESTEIN**, the summit at the crossing of the Schwarzwaldhochstrasse with the street of Baiersbronn in the Rench and the Acher Valleys.

▼ **SPAS OF THE NORTH BLACK FOREST** are, to name a few, Bad Teinach (upper left), Bad Wildbad (lower left) and Bad Liebenzell (lower right).

▼ **EBERSTEIN CASTLE** is a grand neo-Gothic castle complex near Gernsbach in the Murg Valley (upper right). The legendary "Grafensprung" below the castle is freely accessible. According to the story, the Count Wolf of Eberstein spurred on his horse upon these cliffs, in order to get away from Count Eberhard of Württemberg, who was in pursuit; while the horse had not survived the Murg Valley, Wolf managed to escape without harm. Recalling the brave ride is the vineyard location named "Schloss Ebersteiner Grafensprung."

◄ DIE GOTISCHEN RUINEN des 1191 gegründeten Prämonstratenserklosters Allerheiligen liegen oberhalb der Büttensteiner Wasserfälle im Lierbachtal. – In der Ruine des Benediktinerinnenklosters Frauenalb (oben rechts) finden heute Konzerte statt. Nach der Gründung von Frauenalb um 1180 wurde das talaufwärts gelegene Zisterzienserkloster Alba in „Alba dominorum" (Herrenalb) umbenannt, heute Bad Herrenalb. – In den Ruinen des Benediktinerklosters Hirsau finden im Sommer die Klosterspiele Hirsau statt.

▼ DER HOHLOHSEE (rechts unten) ist ein Hochmoorsee im Natur- und Waldschutzgebiet Kaltenbronn.

▼ AUF DEM SCHLOSSBERG der „Goldstadt" Pforzheim, der Metropole des Nordschwarzwalds, thront die im Kern romanische Schlosskirche, in der mehrere badische Markgrafen ihre letzte Ruhestätte gefunden haben.

◄ THE GOTHIC RUINS of the Prémontré All Saints monastery, founded in 1191, are located up from the Büttenstein Waterfalls in the Lierbach Valley. – The ruins of the Benedictine nunnery Frauenalb (upper right) form the backdrop for classical concerts. After the founding of the monastery Frauenalb around 1180, the close Cistercian monastery Alba was renamed "Alba dominorum" (Herrenalb), today Bad Herrenalb. – In summer, the ruins of the Benedictine monastery Hirsau form the backdrop for the monastery stage plays of Hirsau and the Aurelius concerts.

▼ THE HOHLOHSEE (below right) is a raised bog lake in the nature and forest preserve area of Kaltenbronn.

▼ THE SCHLOSSBERG of the "Golden City" of Pforzheim is dominated by the Romanesque castle church, in which many Badish Margraves have found their last resting place.

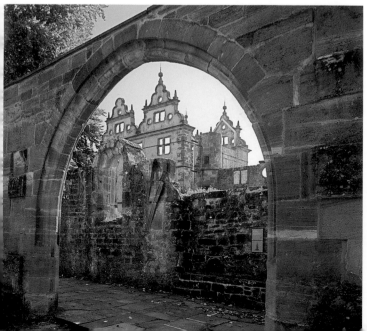

Unser komplettes Programm:

www.bruckmann.de

Produktmanagement: Susanne Caesar
Grundlayout: Dr. Alex Klubertanz, München
Satz: medienpartner.münchen
Redaktion: medienpartner.münchen, Dr. Reinhard Pietsch, München
Texte: Bernhard Pollmann, Emden-Larrelt
Übersetzung ins Englische: William Keller, Augsburg
Repro: Cromika s.a.s., Verona
Umschlaggestaltung: Nina Andritzky unter Verwendung eines Fotos der Bildagentur Huber
Kartografie: Astrid Fischer-Leitl, München
Herstellung: Bettina Schippel
Printed in Slovenia by MKT Print, Ljubljana

Alle Angaben dieses Werkes wurden vom Autor sorgfältig recherchiert und auf den aktuellen Stand gebracht sowie vom Verlag geprüft. Für die Richtigkeit der Angaben kann jedoch keine Haftung übernommen werden. Für Hinweise und Anregungen sind wir jederzeit dankbar. Bitte richten Sie diese an:

Bruckmann Verlag
Postfach 40 02 09
D–80702 München
E-Mail: lektorat@bruckmann.de

Bildnachweis:
Umschlagvorderseite: Waldau, Titisee-Neustadt
Umschlagrückseite: von oben nach unten: Schiltach, Kurhaus in Baden-Baden, Mädchen in Tracht, Winterstimmung am Ruhestein

 Alle Abbildungen des Umschlags und des Innenteils stammen von der Bildagentur Huber, Garmisch-Partenkirchen.

BILDAGENTUR
HUBER

Die Deutsche Nationalbibliothek –
CIP-Einheitsaufnahme
Ein Titelsatz für diese Publikation ist bei Der Deutschen Nationalbibliothek erhältlich.
© 2008 Bruckmann Verlag GmbH, München
ISBN 978-3-7654-4622-1